CONTENTS

HOW TO USE THE CD ACCOMPANIMENT:

A MELODY CUE APPEARS ON THE RIGHT CHANNEL ONLY. IF YOUR CD PLAYER HAS A BALANCE ADJUSTMENT, YOU CAN ADJUST THE VOLUME OF THE MELODY BY TURNING DOWN THE RIGHT CHANNEL.

THE CD IS PLAYABLE ON ANY CD PLAYER, AND IS ALSO ENHANCED SO MAC AND PC USERS CAN ADJUST THE RECORDING TO ANY TEMPO WITHOUT CHANGING THE PITCH.

Series Artwork, Fox Trademarks and Logos
TM and © 2010 Twentieth Century Fox Film Corporation.
All Rights Reserved.

ISBN 978-1-4234-9502-4

7777 W. BLUEMOUND RD. P.O. BOX 13819 MILWAUKEE, WI 53213

Visit Hal Leonard Online at
www.halleonard.com

◆ ALONE

Clarinet

Words and Music by BILLY STEINBERG
and TOM KELLY

❷ BUST YOUR WINDOWS

Clarinet

Words and Music by JAZMINE SULLIVAN,
SALAAM REMI and DEANDRE WAY

❸ AND I AM TELLING YOU I'M NOT GOING

from DREAMGIRLS

Clarinet

Music by HENRY KRIEGER
Lyric by TOM EYEN

◆ DANCING WITH MYSELF

Clarinet

Words and Music by BILLY IDOL
and TONY JAMES

◆⁵ IMAGINE

CLARINET

Words and Music by
JOHN LENNON

◆ DEFYING GRAVITY

CLARINET

Words and Music by
STEPHEN SCHWARTZ

◆ 7 DON'T STOP BELIEVIN'

Clarinet

Words and Music by STEVE PERRY,
NEAL SCHON and JONATHAN CAIN

KEEP HOLDING ON

from the Twentieth Century Fox Motion Picture ERAGON

Clarinet

Words and Music by AVRIL LAVIGNE
and LUKAS GOTTWALD

◆9 LEAN ON ME

Clarinet

Words and Music by
BILL WITHERS

⑩ MY LIFE WOULD SUCK WITHOUT YOU

Clarinet

Words and Music by LUKASZ GOTTWALD,
MAX MARTIN and CLAUDE KELLY

◆11 SWEET CAROLINE

Clarinet

Words and Music by
NEIL DIAMOND

NO AIR

Clarinet

Words and Music by JAMES FAUNTLEROY II,
STEVEN RUSSELL, HARVEY MASON, JR.,
DAMON THOMAS and ERIK GRIGGS

⓭ TAKE A BOW

Words and Music by SHAFFER SMITH,
TOR ERIK HERMANSEN and MIKKEL ERIKSEN

CLARINET

◆ TAKING CHANCES

Clarinet

Words and Music by DAVE STEWART
and KARA DioGUARDI

23

◆15 TRUE COLORS

Clarinet

Words and Music by BILLY STEINBERG
and TOM KELLY